The Best 50
FROZEN COCKTAILS

Hannah Suhr

Bristol Publishing Enterprises
Hayward, California

Printed in the United States of America.
ISBN: 1-55867-333-4
ISBN 13: 978-1-55867-333-5

Cover design: Frank J. Paredes
Cover photography: John A. Benson
Food Styling: Randy Mon

FROZEN SUMMER FLAVORS

Frozen cocktails are icy, light and clean. Fresh fruits and herbs are abundant during the summer and make an excellent foundation for cocktails. Puree them with ice. Jazz them up with spices, teas, ginger and flower waters. Deepen flavors with chocolates and espressos. Sweeten them elegantly with fruit nectars, honey and vanilla. Enrich them with fresh cream.

So that no one will be left behind in this delicious undertaking, we've included a number of nonalcoholic treats throughout the book. These are not your average cocktails. These are hammock-swinging, toes-in-the-sand, bird-chirping, local-farm-fruit- stand salutes to the languid, lazy, luscious days of summer.

SIMPLE SYRUP

Sweeteners such as white sugar, brown sugar and honey can be difficult to dissolve into cold liquids. The result can be a flavor and texture disaster. Keeping simple syrups on hand is helpful not only for cocktails, but for iced teas, lemonades or limeades, desserts and quick dessert sauces, and they're a breeze to make — hence the name.

1 cup water
1 cup granulated sugar, brown sugar or honey

Place water and sugar in a small saucepan over medium heat. Bring to a boil, stirring constantly. As soon as the sugar is completely dissolved, remove syrup from the heat and set aside to cool. Syrup will keep, tightly covered in the refrigerator, for weeks.

FREEZING INGREDIENTS

The best route to a thick and flavorful frozen drink is to pre-freeze the ingredients. This allows you to add less ice, which is ultimately just adding water. Use store-bought frozen fruit, or even better, lay fresh fruit in small chunks on cookie sheets. Once frozen, add to drinks or store in plastic freezer bags in the freezer. Teas and juices can be made into ice cubes and stored in the same way. This simple extra step ensures the best frozen cocktails possible.

MORTAR AND PESTLE

Many drink recipes call for muddling fruits, fresh herbs and spices in the bottom of a glass before adding liquid. This process can be difficult. You can damage your glass, ingredients don't always mix properly and it's not easy to reach down there with your utensil. A much easier option is to use a mortar and pestle to mix your ingredients into a paste. Store this paste in a covered container for the evening, and then spoon out your mixture into a shaker or blender for each batch.

If you don't have a mortar and pestle, mound your fresh herbs and zest on a cutting board, sprinkle with sugar and mash with the flat side of a knife. The sugar acts as an abrasive, helping to quickly turn the mixture into a paste. Scrape the paste into a jar and set aside until you need it. This small bit of advance work will keep your drinks flowing smoothly all evening.

FRESH WHIPPED CREAM

Makes about 4 cups

Chilled cream whips faster, so don't take that container out of the fridge until you're ready to go. If you have time, you can even chill your bowl and beaters. Whipped cream won't hold its shape forever, so prepare this treat no more than a few hours in advance.

1 pint heavy whipping cream
1 tsp. vanilla extract
¼ cup sugar

Place cream and vanilla in a large bowl and beat with an electric mixer on high, adding sugar about 1 tablespoon at a time, until soft peaks form. Take care not to overmix or it will begin to separate. Store, covered, in the refrigerator until ready to use.

ABOUT GRANITAS

A granita is a granular Sicilian ice with a sugar-syrup base, usually flavored with fruit purée, coffee, or wine. The liquid mixture is poured into a shallow glass baking dish and scraped with a fork every half hour, fluffing the ice into a scoopable consistency. Adding just the right amount of alcohol keeps ice crystals separate and leaves the ice easy to scrape. Add too much and your mixture won't freeze, so take care to measure ingredients properly.

Granitas can be made without alcohol as well; the texture will be a bit icier but the flavor will still be fabulous. Adding a tablespoon or two of lemon or lime juice to nonalcoholic fruit granitas enhances the flavor of the fruit.

Granitas, with or without alcohol, are best served within a day or so.

SAUVIGNON MINT GRANITA

Makes 4–6 servings

The sugar and mint turn the bright crisp grape flavor into an elegant dessert ice. Garnish with fresh mint and serve in a delicate wineglass or a martini glass.

1 cup *Simple Syrup*, page 2
2 cups Sauvignon Blanc
1/2 cup minced fresh mint leaves
1 tsp. grated lemon zest

Combine all ingredients in a shallow glass baking dish and place in freezer. Scrape with a fork every half-hour to break up ice crystals until granita is completely frozen (about 4 hours). Be sure to scrape down to the bottom to ensure the mint and zest are distributed evenly. Serve in martini glasses.

BLACK TEA AND HONEY GRANITA

Makes 4–6 servings

The flavor of black tea becomes elegant and complex with the addition of honey, lemon zest and a top-shelf vodka.

1 cup *Simple Syrup,* page 2, made with honey
1½ cups cold brewed black tea
½ cup vodka
1 tsp. grated lemon zest, plus additional for garnish

Combine all ingredients except garnish in a shallow glass baking dish and place in freezer. Scrape with a fork every half-hour to break up ice crystals until granita is completely frozen (about 4 hours). Be sure to scrape down to the bottom to ensure the zest is distributed evenly. Serve in champagne glasses with a sprinkling of lemon zest.

BASIL FIG GRANITA

Makes 4–6 servings

Savory basil complements the honey-sweet fig elegantly, and Pinot Gris (or Pinot Grigio) offers a clean background.

1 cup *Simple Syrup,* page 2, made with honey
2 cups Pinot Gris
1/2 cup minced fresh basil leaves

1 cup fresh figs, trimmed and quartered
2–3 fresh figs, halved, for garnish
honey, for garnish

Place all ingredients except garnishes in a food processor workbowl and process until puréed. Pour mixture into a shallow glass baking dish and place in freezer. Scrape with a fork every half-hour to break up ice crystals until granita is completely frozen (about 4 hours). Be sure to scrape down to the bottom to ensure the fruit and herbs are distributed evenly. Serve granita in glasses topped with halved figs and a drizzle of honey.

MACCHIATO GRANITA

Macchiato means to mark or to stain. Traditional Italian macchiatos mark espresso with a small amount of foamed milk. This version marks sweet and icy espresso granita with a touch of whipped cream. Heaven.

1 cup *Simple Syrup,* page 2
1 cup cold brewed espresso
$1/2$ cup vodka
Fresh Whipped Cream, page 5, for garnish

Combine all ingredients except whipped cream in a shallow glass baking dish and place in freezer. Scrape with a fork every half-hour to break up ice crystals until granita is completely frozen (about 4 hours). Serve in martini glasses with a small dollop of Fresh Whipped Cream.

HONEY ALMOND GRANITA

A classic, simple combination everyone loves. Serve this granita with amaretti cookies after an Italian summer meal. Find almond milk in health food stores.

1/2 cup *Simple Syrup,* page 2, made with honey
1 cup amaretto liqueur
2 cups almond milk

Combine all ingredients in a shallow glass baking dish and place in freezer. Scrape with a fork every half-hour to break up ice crystals until granita is completely frozen (about 4 hours). Serve in martini glasses.

MOCHA GRANITA

Makes 4–6 servings

Nothing beats the combination of coffee, milk and chocolate. Enjoy this granita whenever the craving hits — but you may want to omit the vodka at breakfast! Use top-quality chocolate syrup for the best flavor.

1 cup cold brewed coffee	1/2 cup vodka
1 cup low-fat or whole milk	chocolate-covered espresso
1/4 cup chocolate syrup	beans, for garnish

Combine all ingredients except garnish in a shallow glass baking dish and place in freezer. Scrape with a fork every half-hour to break up ice crystals until granita is completely frozen (about 4 hours). Serve in martini glasses. Garnish with chocolate-covered espresso beans.

MANGO MINT GRANITA

Makes 4–6 servings

Sweet and cool, this granita is excellent for any summer gathering. You may use peaches if mangos are unavailable.

1 cup mango puree or nectar
1/2 cup minced fresh mint leaves
1/2 cup light rum
1/2 cup *Simple Syrup,* page 2
1 cup water
4–6 sprigs fresh mint, for garnish

Combine all ingredients except garnish in a shallow glass baking dish and place in freezer. Scrape with a fork every half-hour to break up ice crystals until granita is completely frozen (about 4 hours). Be sure to scrape down to the bottom to ensure mint is distributed evenly. Serve in martini glasses, garnished with fresh mint.

LIMONCELLO GRANITA

A sweet-tart natural lemon liqueur from Italy, limoncello has been gathering popularity lately as a fashionable cocktail. Its balance is excellent and needs no more than water and a little fresh zest. Add a splash of sparkling water to each glass, if you wish.

1 cup limoncello liqueur
2 cups water
2–3 tbs. grated lemon zest
4–6 sprigs fresh mint, for garnish, optional

Combine all ingredients except garnish in a shallow glass baking dish and place in freezer. Scrape with a fork every half-hour to break up ice crystals until granita is completely frozen (about 4 hours). Serve in martini glasses garnished with fresh mint.

PINK GRAPEFRUIT ANISE GRANITA

Makes 4–6 servings

Tart and sweet, this granita is unexpected and sophisticated. Garnish with a star anise to identify the flavor, as anise may catch some people off-guard.

2 cups pink grapefruit juice
1/2 cup *Simple Syrup,* page 2
1/4 cup anise liqueur (anisette or Pernod)

1/2 cup vodka
4–6 whole star anise, for garnish
4–6 sprigs fresh mint, for garnish

Combine all ingredients except garnishes in a shallow glass baking dish and place in freezer. Scrape with a fork every half-hour to break up ice crystals until granita is completely frozen (about 4 hours). Serve in martini glasses garnished with star anise and fresh mint.

GREEN TEA AND MINT GRANITA

Subtle, refreshing and full of antioxidants, this simple granita with an Asian meal. Use clear, filtered sake (the most common type), as opposed to the sweeter, cloudy unfiltered sake.

2 cups cold brewed green tea
1/2 cup minced fresh mint leaves
1 cup sake
4–6 sprigs fresh mint, for garnish

Combine all ingredients except garnish in a shallow glass baking dish and place in freezer. Scrape with a fork every half-hour to break up ice crystals until granita is completely frozen (about 4 hours). Be sure to scrape down to the bottom to ensure the mint is distributed evenly. Serve in martini glasses garnished with fresh mint.

ICETINIS (FROZEN MARTINIS)

Martinis are traditionally made with gin or vodka and dry vermouth. New twists on the martini are now popping up every-
where. The following frozen versions are slushy and pile perfectly
into a traditional martini glass, the sexiest bar glass hands down.
Call them icetinis and be sure to call on them often.

CLASSIC ICETINI

Makes 1 serving

A twist on the quintessential cocktail. Serve with classic garnishes: olives, a lemon twist, cocktail onions on toothpicks.

1 oz. vodka
few drops dry vermouth
1 cup crushed ice

Combine all ingredients in a blender container and mix on high until slushy. Serve immediately in a martini glass.

ESPRESSO ICETINI

This is a dark, intense cocktail. Espresso should be made ahead of time and set on ice until chilled. If necessary strong coffee may be substituted.

1 shot (about 1½ oz.) cold brewed espresso
1 oz. vodka
1 cup crushed ice
heavy cream, for garnish, optional

Combine all ingredients except garnish in a blender container and mix on high until slushy. Drink straight or drizzle with a little heavy cream before serving in a martini glass.

LAVENDER ICETINI

Makes 1 serving

Edible (culinary grade) lavender blossoms can be found in specialty gourmet shops, herb shops and online. If desired you can add one drop of red and one drop of blue food coloring to a large batch of icetinis. The pale lavender color does an excellent job of identifying this unusual cocktail.

1 tsp. edible lavender blossoms
1 oz. vodka
1 oz. *Simple Syrup,* page 2
1 cup crushed ice

Combine all ingredients in a blender container and mix on high until slushy. Serve immediately in a martini glass.

WATERMELON ICETINI

Makes 1 serving

Freezing the melon ahead of time creates a denser, more flavorful cocktail than adding ice to fresh fruit. Cube fruit and freeze on cookie sheets. Use immediately or store in freezer bags.

1/2 cup peeled, seeded, cubed frozen watermelon
1 oz. vodka
1 thin wedge watermelon, for garnish

Combine all ingredients except garnish in a blender container and mix on high until slushy. Serve immediately in a martini glass. Garnish with a watermelon wedge spliced to the edge of the glass.

PINEAPPLE ICETINI

Makes 1 serving

Freezing the pineapple ahead of time means you can skip the ice — and a possibility of a watery drink. Cube fruit and freeze on cookie sheets. Use immediately or store in freezer bags.

$1/2$ cup peeled, cubed frozen pineapple
1 oz. vodka
1 small wedge pineapple, for garnish

Combine all ingredients except garnish in a blender container and mix on high until slushy. Serve immediately in a martini glass. Garnish with a fresh pineapple wedge spliced to the edge of the glass.

SAKE ICETINI

Makes 1 serving

A frozen slushy cucumber drink is quite unusual and the most refreshing thing you'll ever find. Peel and cube a cucumber and freeze on a cookie sheet. Use immediately or store in freezer bags. Clear filtered sake —the most common type — will be best here.

½ cup sake
½ cup peeled, seeded, cubed frozen cucumber
1 slice cucumber, for garnish
1 sprig fresh mint, for garnish, optional

Combine all ingredients except garnishes in a blender container er container and mix on high until slushy. Serve immediately in a martini glass. Garnish with a cucumber slice spliced to the edge of the glass and a sprig of fresh mint, if desired.

CHASTE CUCUMBER COOLER

Makes 1 serving

Cucumber is the essence of summer. This slushy, nonalcoholic drink is excellent as an afternoon refresher after a day at the beach.

$1/2$ cup peeled, seeded, cubed frozen cucumber
$1/2$ cup lemonade
1 slice cucumber, for garnish
1 sprig fresh mint, for garnish, optional

Combine all ingredients except garnishes in a blender container-er container and mix on high until slushy. Serve immediately in a jelly jar. Garnish with a cucumber slice spliced to the edge of the glass and a sprig of fresh mint, if desired.

AMARETTO LIME ICETINI

The heady sweetness of amaretto and brown sugar is cut perfectly with fresh lime. This is a beautiful amber cocktail perfect for afternoon lounging on a shady porch with your favorite friends.

1 oz. vodka
1 oz. amaretto
1 oz. fresh lime juice
1 cup crushed ice
1 oz. *Simple Syrup*, page 2, made with brown sugar
1 wedge lime, for garnish

Combine all ingredients except garnish in a blender container and mix on high until slushy. Serve immediately in a martini glass. Garnish with a wedge of lime.

JASMINE HONEYDEW ICETINI

Makes 1 serving

This delicate cocktail is perfect for a summer garden party, complete with straw hats and tea sandwiches.

$^1/_2$ cup cold brewed jasmine tea
$^1/_2$ cup peeled, seeded, cubed frozen honeydew melon
1 oz. vodka
1 thin wedge honeydew, for garnish

Combine all ingredients except garnish in a blender container and mix on high until slushy. Serve in a martini glass and garnish with a wedge of honeydew.

APRICOT ANISE ICETINI

Makes 1 serving

A sharp and floral cocktail savored by the most sophisticated palates. Use only fresh or frozen apricots, not dried, or use peaches in a pinch.

½ cup peeled, pitted, cubed frozen apricots
1 cup crushed ice
1 oz. anise liqueur (anisette or Pernod)
1 slice fresh apricot, for garnish
1 star anise, for garnish

Combine all ingredients except garnishes in a blender container and mix on high until slushy. Serve in a martini glass garnished with a fresh apricot slice and a star anise.

MAYAN CHOCOLATE ICETINI

The unexpected addition of spicy chile brings out the nuances of chocolate's flavors. Use the best quality chocolate syrup you can find, for the ultimate chocolate flavor.

1 oz. chocolate syrup
1/4 tsp. chile powder
1 oz. vodka
1 cup crushed ice
shaved chocolate, for garnish

Combine all ingredients except garnish in a blender container and mix on high until slushy. Serve in a martini glass and garnish with shaved chocolate.

FROJITOS (FROZEN MOJITOS)

Mojitos are traditionally made from rum, sugar, lime juice, fresh mint, soda water and shaved ice. This versatile base lends itself well to many unexpected flavors.

FROJITO PASTE

Muddle ½ cup fresh mint leaves, ¼ cup sugar and the grated zest and juice of 1 lime with a mortar and pestle until a paste forms. Or mash together the mint, sugar and zest on a cutting board with the flat side of a knife. Scrape the paste into a jar and stir in the lime juice. This paste can be used for every frojito recipe, and will keep in the fridge for a day.

CLASSIC FROJITO

Makes 1 serving

Classic mojito flavor is transformed into a slushy summery cocktail. The ultimate refreshment.

1 oz. light rum
1 oz. *Simple Syrup*, page 2
½ tsp. *Frojito Paste*, page 29
1 cup crushed ice
1 splash soda water
1 wedge lime, for garnish

Combine rum, *Simple Syrup*, *Frojito Paste* and ice in a blender container. Blend on high until slushy. Serve in a stemmed glass, top with a splash of soda water and garnish with a wedge of lime.

HOLY MOJITO

Makes 1 serving

With all the lovely mint and lime flavor of the classic, but none of the alcohol, this is an excellent alternative to offer at your next cocktail party.

1 oz. *Simple Syrup*, page 2, made with brown sugar
1 tsp. *Frojito Paste,* page 29
1 cup crushed ice
½ cup soda water, plus more for garnish
1 wedge lime, for garnish

Combine all ingredients except garnishes in a blender container and blend on high until slushy. Serve in a stemmed glass, top with a splash of soda water and garnish with a wedge of lime.

MELON MINT FROJITO

Makes 1 serving

Melon adds a delicate sweetness and smooth texture to this crisp cocktail. Stick with either all cantaloupe or all honeydew for the best color. Any other summer melon such as Cranshaw may also be used.

1 cup peeled, seeded, cubed frozen cantaloupe or honeydew
1 oz. light rum
1 oz. *Simple Syrup,* page 2
½ tsp. *Frojito Paste,* page 29
1 splash soda water
1 wedge lime, for garnish

Combine melon, rum, *Simple Syrup* and *Frojito Paste* in a blender container. Blend on high until slushy. Serve in a stemmed glass, top with a splash of soda water and garnish with a wedge of lime.

CHERRY VANILLA REFRESHER

This light, sweet and bubbly drink is a twist on the old-school Shirley Temple. Kids and nostalgic adults alike will adore it.

$\frac{1}{2}$ cup cream soda
$\frac{1}{2}$ cup crushed ice
1 tbs. grenadine
1 maraschino cherry, for garnish

Combine all ingredients except garnish in a blender container and blend on high until slushy. Serve in a tall glass and garnish with a cherry.

STRAWBERRY MINT FROJITO

Makes 1 serving

Strawberries pair perfectly with brown sugar and mint. Freeze your own fresh berries rather than using the frozen variety when you can. Choose local whenever possible as they are picked ripe. Organic is also a good bet as the skin of these berries is very thin.

1 cup sliced frozen strawberries
1 oz. light rum
½ oz. *Simple Syrup*, page 2, made with brown sugar
½ tsp. *Frojito Paste*, page 29
1 splash soda water
1 wedge lime, for garnish

Combine strawberries, rum, *Simple Syrup* and *Frojito Paste* in a blender container. Blend on high until slushy. Serve in a stemmed glass, top with soda water and garnish with wedge of lime.

GINGER MINT FROJITO

Spicy and clean, fresh ginger is the star of this intense summer cocktail. Just a touch does the trick.

1 tsp. grated fresh ginger	1 cup crushed ice
½ tsp. *Frojito Paste*, page 29	1 splash soda water
1 oz. light rum	1 sprig fresh mint
½ oz. *Simple Syrup*, page 2	1 wedge lime, for garnish

Mash the ginger with *Frojito Paste* until well mixed. Combine paste with rum, *Simple Syrup* and ice in a blender container and mix on high until slushy. Serve in a martini glass, splash with soda water and garnish with fresh mint and a wedge of lime.

POMEGRANATE MINT FROJITO

Makes 1 serving

The vibrant, tart juice of pomegranate seeds (now available in most grocery stores) is packed with antioxidants.

1 oz. pomegranate juice
1 oz. light rum
1/2 oz. *Simple Syrup,* page 2
1/2 tsp. *Frojito Paste,* page 29
1 cup crushed ice
1 splash soda water
1 sprig fresh mint, for garnish

Combine pomegranate juice, rum, *Simple Syrup*, *Frojito Paste* and ice in a blender container. Blend on high until slushy. Serve in a stemmed glass, top with a splash of soda water and garnish with fresh mint.

FROZEN DAIQUIRIS

A cocktail of rum, lemon or lime juice and sugar, the daiquiri is usually served frozen, and often with the addition of fruit. Try some new and unexpected additions to this classic slushy drink at your next gathering.

CLASSIC DAIQUIRI

Makes 1 serving

Simple and bright, this classic frozen cocktail is perfect anytime.

1 oz. light rum
½ oz. lime juice
1 oz. *Simple Syrup,* page 2
1 cup crushed ice
1 wedge lime, for garnish

Combine all ingredients except garnish in a blender container and mix on high until slushy. Serve in a glass with a wedge of lime.

HONEY ROSEWATER DAIQUIRI

Makes 1 serving

Sweet and floral, this is a delicate cocktail. A single drop of red food coloring in a batch of cocktails offers a pale pink color identifying the rose. Most health food stores will carry rosewater, but do make sure you use the type intended for food.

1 oz. light rum
½ oz. *Simple Syrup,* page 2
½ oz. edible rosewater
1 tsp. lemon juice
1 cup crushed ice

Combine all ingredients in a blender container and mix on high until slushy. Serve in a jelly jar.

SUMMER MELON DAIQUIRI

This simple and fresh summer cocktail can be made with any type of melon you can find. Go local, go exotic, but buy what's fresh, firm and sweet-smelling.

1/2 cup peeled, seeded, cubed frozen melon
1 oz. light rum
1/2 oz. *Simple Syrup*, page 2
1 tsp. lemon juice
1 cup crushed ice
1 small wedge melon, for garnish

Combine all ingredients except garnish in a blender container and mix on high until slushy. Serve in a glass and garnish with a melon wedge.

GREEN TEA DAIQUIRI

Makes 1 serving

Excellent with sushi rolls and edamame (fresh soybeans), this simple summer cocktail is refreshing and full of antioxidants.

1 oz. cold brewed green tea
1 oz. light rum
$\frac{1}{2}$ oz. *Simple Syrup*, page 2
1 tsp. lemon juice
1 cup crushed ice
1 strip lemon zest, for garnish

Combine all ingredients except garnish in a blender container and mix on high until slushy. Serve in a glass and garnish with lemon zest.

OOLONG TEA DAIQUIRI

Most commonly found in Chinese restaurants, oolong tea has a very distinct earthy flavor. Serve this cocktail with your favorite Chinese takeout.

1 oz. cold brewed oolong tea
1 oz. light rum
1/2 oz. *Simple Syrup*, page 2
1 tsp. lemon juice
1 cup crushed ice
1 strip lemon zest, for garnish

Combine all ingredients except garnish in a blender container and mix on high until slushy. Serve in a glass and garnish with lemon zest.

FROZEN COLADAS

Coladas are slushy mixed drinks made of rum, cream of coconut and ice, the most popular being the piña (or pineapple) colada. Coconut blends well with many other flavors. Substitute low-fat cream of coconut in any of these coladas if desired, as the traditional variety is quite decadent. Cream of coconut is available in the international foods aisle of most supermarkets. Serve coladas at a luau or as a dessert drink on a hot summer's night.

CLASSIC PINEAPPLE COLADA

Makes 1 serving

Everyone loves a piña colada. Go ahead, garnish like crazy with umbrellas, straws and fruit. Pretend you're on a tropical island and the world just disappears.

$\frac{1}{4}$ cup cream of coconut
$\frac{1}{2}$ cup pineapple juice
1 oz. dark rum
1 oz. light rum
1 cup crushed ice

1 maraschino cherry, for
  garnish
1 wedge orange, for garnish
1 wedge pineapple, for garnish

Combine all ingredients except garnishes in a blender container and mix on high until slushy. Serve in a large glass, cover with gaudy garnishes and enjoy.

VIRGIN COLADA

Makes 1 serving

As pure and clean as the undriven snow, this nonalcoholic colada is delectably sweet.

1/4 cup cream of coconut
1/2 cup pineapple juice
1 cup crushed ice
1 maraschino cherry, for garnish
1 wedge orange, for garnish
1 wedge pineapple, for garnish

Combine all ingredients except garnishes in a blender container and mix on high until slushy. Serve in a large glass, cover with garnishes and enjoy.

COFFEE BANANA COLADA

Makes 1 serving

Frozen bananas create the perfect creamy consistency and the addition of coffee makes this one rich and outstanding.

$\frac{1}{4}$ cup cream of coconut
$\frac{1}{2}$ cup cold brewed coffee
1 small frozen banana, peeled and chopped
1 oz. dark rum
1 slice banana, for garnish

Combine all ingredients except garnish in a blender container and mix on high until slushy. Serve in a large glass with a banana slice on the rim.

COCOA COLADA

Makes 1 serving

Chocolate and coconut make an unbeatable combination. Serve this one for dessert topped with Fresh Whipped Cream, *or simply in a tall glass with a straw.*

1/4 cup cream of coconut
1/4 cup chocolate syrup
1/2 cup milk
1 oz. dark rum
1 cup crushed ice
Fresh Whipped Cream, page 5, for garnish
shredded toasted coconut, for garnish

Combine all ingredients except garnishes in a blender container and mix on high until slushy. Serve in a large glass topped with *Fresh Whipped Cream* and toasted coconut.

ALMOND COLADA

Makes 1 serving

Almond and coconut are delicate, naturally sweet flavors. Try topping this one with shaved dark chocolate for a more decadent treat.

1 oz. Frangelico or almond liqueur
1 oz. light rum
1/4 cup cream of coconut
1/2 cup almond milk
1 cup crushed ice
toasted slivered almonds, for garnish

Combine all ingredients except garnish in a blender container and mix on high until slushy. Serve in a large glass, topped with slivered almonds.

AUSTERE ORANGE AMBROSIA SLUSH

Makes 1 serving

This tropical treat is beachy, celebratory and kid-friendly, since we've skipped the alcohol here.

½ cup orange juice
½ cup crushed ice
1 tbs. cream of coconut
1 wedge orange, for garnish
1 maraschino cherry, for garnish

Combine all ingredients except garnishes in a blender container and mix on high until slushy. Serve in a large glass and garnish with an orange wedge and a cherry.

ORANGE COLADA

The Creamsicle, our favorite treat from the ice cream truck, is now for grownups.

¼ cup cream of coconut
1 oz. light rum
½ cup orange juice
1 cup crushed ice
1 wedge orange, for garnish
1 maraschino cherry, for garnish

Combine all ingredients except garnishes in a blender container and mix on high until slushy. Serve in a large glass and garnish with an orange wedge and a cherry.

CHAI TEA COLADA

Makes 1 serving

The rich spicy sweetness of chai tea turns coconut into one heck of a colada. Your guests will flock to this trendy, complex, irresistible cocktail. Prepared chai tea is available in both refrigerated and unrefrigerated cartons in your better grocery stores.

¼ cup cream of coconut
1 oz. dark rum
½ cup prepared cold chai tea
1 cup crushed ice
cinnamon, for garnish

Combine all ingredients except garnish in a blender container and mix on high until slushy. Serve in a large glass and top with a dusting of cinnamon.

VESTAL VANILLA FRAPPE

Simple and delicious, this drink is a low-fat version of a soda shop favorite, a huge hit with kids and great as a light dessert. Try using chocolate or coffee frozen yogurt for variety.

$1/2$ cup vanilla frozen yogurt
$1/2$ cup skim (nonfat) milk
$1/2$ tsp. vanilla extract
$1/4$ tsp. cinnamon

Combine all ingredients in a blender container and mix on high until slushy. Serve in a large glass and sprinkle lightly with cinnamon. Serve with a straw.

MANDARIN CHILE COLADA

Makes 1 serving

Sweet, rich and spicy. Don't freeze the orange segments all together as they will freeze into a solid block and will be difficult to separate and to blend.

1 can (11 oz.) mandarin orange segments
1/4 cup cream of coconut
1 oz. light rum
1 oz. dark rum
chile powder, for garnish

Drain mandarin oranges, reserving the liquid. Spread the orange segments on a cookie sheet and place in freezer until frozen. Combine frozen oranges with cream of coconut, reserved juice and both rums in a blender container and mix on high until slushy. Serve in a large glass, sprinkled with chile powder.

ICEMARYS (FROZEN BLOODY MARYS)

The Bloody Mary is traditionally a Sunday morning brunch drink made from tomato juice and vodka, and flavored with anything from lemon and celery salt to Worcestershire and horseradish. The tremendous flavor combination has been limited by its less than appetizing name and its social relegation to the early hours of the day. Icemarys are slushy versions of this classic cocktail, spiced up and set free. Enjoy them any time of the day or night. They are especially fabulous served alongside a raw bar.

CLASSIC ICEMARY

Makes 1 serving

This slushy version of the classic Bloody Mary is spicy and flavorful, perfect for afternoon cocktail parties.

1 oz. vodka
1/2 cup tomato juice
1/2 tsp. prepared horseradish
1 tsp. lemon juice
1/2 tsp. Worcestershire sauce
1 cup crushed ice
1 celery stalk, for garnish
cracked black pepper, for garnish

Combine all ingredients except garnishes in a blender container and mix on high until slushy. Serve in a tall glass and garnish with celery and pepper. Ingredients may be adjusted to taste.

BLUSHING MARY

Makes 1 serving

This virgin Bloody Mary is classic, healthy and innocent as a blushing bride.

$^1/_2$ cup tomato juice
$^1/_2$ tsp. prepared horseradish
1 tsp. lemon juice
$^1/_2$ tsp. Worcestershire sauce
1 cup crushed ice
1 celery stalk, for garnish
cracked black pepper, for garnish

Combine all ingredients except garnishes in a blender container and mix on high until slushy. Serve in a tall glass and garnish with celery and pepper. Ingredients may be adjusted to taste.

DIRTY ICEMARY

Makes 1 serving

The briny olive flavor complements the savory components of this beverage so well, it's practically a lunch unto itself.

1 oz. vodka
½ cup tomato juice
1 tsp. lemon juice
1 tsp. olive juice/brine
1 cup crushed ice
2 green olives, for garnish
1 celery stalk, for garnish

Combine all ingredients except garnishes in a blender container and mix on high until slushy. Serve in a tall glass and garnish with olives and celery.

RAW BAR ICEMARY

Makes 1 serving

The icy bed of spicy tomato slush makes an obvious pairing for raw bar foods, and is also perfect for a clambake. Use any type of clams, oysters, etc.; be sure shells are scrubbed spotlessly clean.

1 oz. vodka
½ cup Clamato juice (tomato juice and clam broth)
1 tsp. prepared horseradish
1 tsp. lemon juice
½ tsp. Worcestershire sauce
1 cup crushed ice
raw shellfish of choice
1 wedge lemon

Combine vodka, Clamato, horseradish, lemon juice, Worcestershire and ice in a blender container and mix on high until slushy. Add more ice if necessary; the drink should be thick enough to hold up its garnishes. Serve in a wide low glass. Rest raw bar food of choice and a lemon wedge on the surface of the drink.

ROSEMARY ICEMARY

Rosemary combines beautifully with tomatoes. Try this drink with gin instead of vodka for an additional resiny twist.

1 oz. vodka
1/2 cup tomato juice
1 tsp. lemon juice
1 cup crushed ice
1/2 tsp. very finely chopped fresh rosemary
1 sprig fresh rosemary, for garnish
cracked pepper, for garnish

Combine all ingredients except garnishes in a blender container and mix on high until slushy. Serve in a tall glass and garnish with rosemary and pepper.

SPICY SHRIMP ICEMARY

Makes 1 serving

Cocktail sauce—meet cute with cocktail! Use skewered cocktail shrimp in place of the Grilled Shrimp Skewers, *if you wish.*

1 oz. vodka
1/2 cup tomato juice
1 tsp. lemon juice
1 tsp. prepared horseradish

1 cup crushed ice
1 wedge lemon, for garnish
Grilled Shrimp Skewers, below

Combine all ingredients except garnishes in a blender container and mix on high until slushy. Serve in a wide glass garnished with a *Shrimp Skewer,* below, and lemon wedge.

GRILLED SHRIMP SKEWERS

Spear 2 to 3 shrimp on a bamboo skewer. Brush with olive oil and sprinkle with salt, pepper and a dusting of chili powder. Grill until just cooked through and browned, 2 to 3 minutes each side.

LEMONY ICEMARY

Some extra lemon and a little sugar bring sweet, sour and savory together.

1 oz. vodka
½ cup tomato juice
1 tbs. lemon juice
1 tsp. grated lemon zest
1 tbs. *Simple Syrup*, page 2
1 cup crushed ice
1 wedge lemon, for garnish

Combine all ingredients except garnish in a blender container and mix on high until slushy. Serve in a tall glass and garnish with a lemon wedge.

FROZEN MARGARITAS

Margaritas are traditionally made with tequila, lime juice and orange liqueur, and often served with a salted rim. Although still often served on the rocks, the most popular margarita is a frozen margarita. The following twists on the classic cocktail are all slushy and may be served with or without salt. To salt the rim of a glass, fill a saucer with salt, rub a lemon or lime wedge on the rim of a glass, and immediately dip into the salt.

CLASSIC FROZEN MARGARITA

Makes 1 serving

Cool and refreshing, this is a perfect summer drink.

1 oz. tequila
1/2 oz. Cointreau or Triple Sec
1 oz. lime juice
1/2 oz. *Simple Syrup*, page 2
1 cup crushed ice
salt for rim, optional
1 wedge lime, for garnish
1 wedge orange, for garnish

Combine all ingredients except garnishes in a blender container and mix on high until slushy. Serve in a wide rimmed glass, salted or unsalted, and garnish with lime and orange wedges.

PINK GRAPEFRUIT FROZEN MARGARITA

Makes 1 serving

The grapefruit provides sweetness and acidity and works perfectly with the traditional ingredients. Replacing sugar with honey in the Simple Syrup adds complexity and brings all the flavors together smoothly.

/₂ cup pink grapefruit juice
1 oz. tequila
¹/₂ oz. Cointreau or Triple Sec
1 cup crushed ice

¹/₂ oz. *Simple Syrup*, page 2,
   made with honey
salt for rim, optional
1 wedge grapefruit, for garnish

Combine all ingredients except garnish in a blender container and mix on high until slushy. Serve in a wide rimmed glass, salted or unsalted, and garnish with a pink grapefruit wedge.

HONEYDEW FROZEN MARGARITA

Makes 1 serving

Honeydew mellows out the traditional margarita, resulting in a smooth and palatable cocktail, even for those who claim they don't like margaritas.

½ cup peeled, seeded, cubed frozen honeydew melon
1 oz. tequila
½ oz. Cointreau or Triple Sec
1 oz. lime juice
½ oz. *Simple Syrup,* page 2
salt for rim, optional
1 wedge lime, for garnish

Combine all ingredients except garnish in a blender container and mix on high until slushy. Serve in a wide rimmed glass, salted or unsalted, and garnish with a wedge of lime.

STRAWBERRY FROZEN MARGARITA

Makes 1 serving

An alternative to the strawberry daiquiri, this cocktail is more complex and less syrupy. Use fresh strawberries you freeze yourself whenever possible; the flavor is completely different from frozen.

½ cup sliced frozen strawberries
1 oz. tequila
½ oz. Cointreau or Triple Sec
1 oz. lime juice
½ oz. *Simple Syrup*, page 2
salt for rim, optional
1 fresh strawberry, for garnish
1 wedge lime, for garnish

Combine all ingredients except garnishes in a blender container and mix on high until slushy. Serve in a wide rimmed glass, salted or unsalted, garnish with a strawberry and a lime wedge.

PEACH FROZEN MARGARITA

Although fresh ripe peaches, peeled and frozen by hand, are superior, frozen peaches are an acceptable substitute.

$^1/_2$ cup frozen sliced peaches
1 oz. tequila
$^1/_2$ oz. Cointreau or Triple Sec
1 oz. lime juice
$^1/_2$ oz. *Simple Syrup,* page 2
1 slice fresh peach, for garnish
1 wedge lime, for garnish

Combine all ingredients except garnishes in a blender container and mix on high until slushy. Serve in a wide rimmed glass, garnished with a peach slice and a wedge of lime.

JALAPEÑO FROZEN MARGARITA

The quintessential "hot" and cold cocktail. Be sure to remove the seeds and ribs from the pepper as they can be painfully hot — unless, of course, you like it that way. And of course use freshly squeezed lime juice every time.

1 tsp. diced jalapeño pepper,
    seeds and ribs removed
1 oz. tequila
½ oz. Cointreau or Triple Sec
1 oz. lime juice
½ oz. *Simple Syrup,* page 2
1 cup crushed ice
salt for rim, optional
1 wedge lime, for garnish

Combine all ingredients except garnish in a blender container and mix on high until slushy. Serve in a wide rimmed glass, salted or unsalted, and garnish with a lime wedge.

CORIANDER-ORANGE MARGARITA

Here's an unusual flavor combination most often found in the brewing of white Belgian ales. Coriander has a sweet-spicy taste that blends well with the bitter orange. Use ground coriander if you can't find whole seeds.

½ tsp. coriander seeds, crushed
1 tbs. bitter orange marmalade
1 oz. tequila
1 oz. lime juice
1 cup crushed ice
salt for rim, optional
1 wedge orange, for garnish

Combine all ingredients except garnish in a blender container and mix on high until slushy. Serve in a wide rimmed glass, salted or unsalted, and garnish with an orange wedge.

ICEMOPOLITANS (ICED COSMOPOLITANS)

The popular cosmopolitan not only has a very fashionable name but also very palatable sweet-tart flavors (cranberry and lime) that cut the taste of the alcohol. Once served in their traditional martini glass, cosmos make the ideal girly drink. These icy versions served with new splashes and garnishes may actually outdo their original appeal.

CLASSIC ICEMOPOLITAN

Makes 1 serving

Tart, sweet and strong, just like you.

1 oz. vodka
2 oz. cranberry juice
½ oz. Cointreau
1 cup crushed ice
1 wedge lime, for garnish

Combine all ingredients except garnish in a blender container and mix on high until slushy. Serve in a martini glass with a wedge of lime.

TANGERINE ICEMOPOLITAN

A little like a Madras (vodka, cranberry and orange juice), but much, much cooler. Bottled tangerine juice may be substituted, but fresh is best.

1 oz. vodka
1 oz. cranberry juice
1 oz. fresh tangerine juice
1 tsp. grated tangerine zest
1 cup crushed ice
1 slice tangerine, for garnish

Combine all ingredients except garnish in a blender container and mix on high until slushy. Serve in a martini glass with a tangerine slice.

RASPBERRY ICEMOPOLITAN

Makes 1 serving

A sweet-tart blood-red cocktail that's especially fit for a girl's night out. Earmark the page to break out next February for the single girls' anti-Valentine's Day cocktail party. Of course, it's a good pro-Valentine's Day drink too, if you have a sweetheart.

1 oz. vodka
1/2 cup frozen raspberries
1 oz. cranberry juice
1/2 oz. Cointreau
1 wedge lime, for garnish

Combine all ingredients except garnish in a blender container and mix on high until slushy. Serve in a martini glass and garnish with a lime wedge.

IMMACULATE BLACK CURRANT ICE

An elegant nonalcoholic slushy cocktail, this is just the thing for designated drivers who want to be included in the party. If black currant juice isn't available, try pomegranate or raspberry juice.

$^1/_2$ cup black currant juice
$^1/_2$ cup crushed ice
1 tbs. *Simple Syrup*, page 2, made with honey
1 sprig fresh mint, for garnish

Combine all ingredients except garnish in a blender container and mix on high until slushy. Serve in a martini glass and garnish with a sprig of mint.

GINGER ICEMOPOLITAN

Sultry and sophisticated, ginger works incredibly well with the cranberry juice (think orange-ginger cranberry sauce).

1 oz. vodka
2 oz. cranberry juice
1/2 oz. Cointreau
1/2 tsp. fresh grated ginger
1 cup crushed ice
1 slice candied ginger, for garnish
1 wedge orange, for garnish

Combine all ingredients except garnishes in a blender container and mix on high until slushy. Serve in a martini glass garnished with a slice of candied ginger and an orange wedge.

INDEX